Hampshire Railv

on old picture ɩ

Andrew Swiπ

1. Aldershot. In 1854, when war broke out in the Crimea, the government bought a large tract of heathland near Alder Shott (its name meaning alder woodland) for a military camp. Within a few years, a sleepy village was transformed into a bustling town, but it did not get its own station until 1870. The yellow-brick station, which harks back to Tite's London & Southampton buildings of 30 years earlier (and with some very nice ironwork), has hardly changed since this postcard was published.

Designed and published by
Reflections of a Bygone Age,
Keyworth, Nottingham 2003

Printed by Adlard Print &
Reprographics Ltd, Ruddington

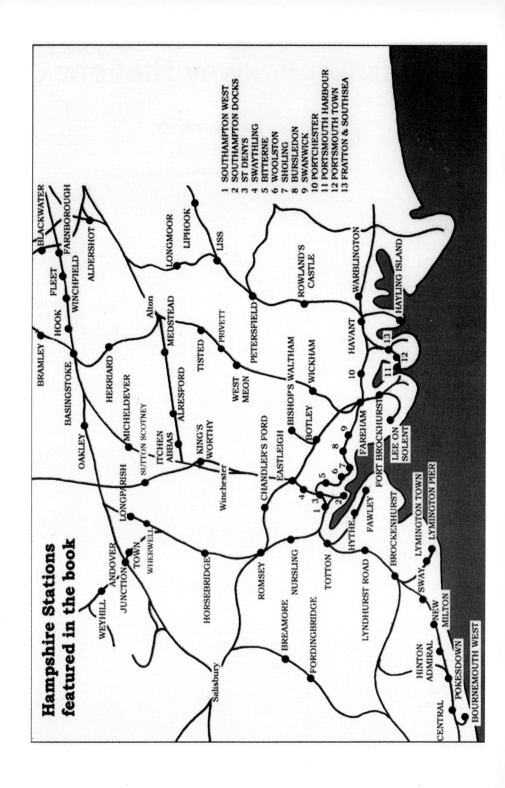

2. Alresford. Many stations in this book have either disappeared or changed beyond all recognition. In one corner of the county, however, strenuous efforts been made to turn the clock back. At Alresford, the terminus of the Watercress Line, the railway scene of half a century ago has been recreated with painstaking attention to detail. In the process, however, all sense of the railway as a functional entity has been lost. What would the folks on this card think if they knew that, a century hence, the view would look much the same, and the trains would still run, but all the passengers would be travelling, not because they wanted to go somewhere, but simply for fun? Card published by Terry Hunt of Basingstoke.

Andover Junction.

3. Andover Junction. The railway reached Andover from Basingstoke in 1854 and was extended to Salisbury three years later. Eventually the route became part of the LSWR's main line to the West of England. Andover later became a junction, with lines north to Cheltenham and south to Romsey, but these closed in 1964. The main line through Andover is still busy and the scene on this card is immediately recognisable today. Although the signalbox, the goods sidings on the right, and the central tracks have gone, the station buildings are still there, as are the sidings on the left. This postcard came from the prolific Southampton publishers Cosser.

ANDOVER TOWN STATION & MOTOR TRAIN

4. Andover Town. Corrugated iron was clearly in fashion when Andover Town, on the line from Andover Junction to Romsey, opened in 1865. The line was built on the bed of the Andover Canal, which probably accounted for its nickname - the 'Sprat & Winkle Line'. Andover Town station was built on - and obliterated - the town's canal wharf. Although the line was promoted as a major through route between the Midlands and the South, steam railmotors like the one on this card were more than adequate for most of the services that ran along it. The line closed in 1964 and virtually no trace of Andover Town station remains today.

5. Basingstoke. The London & Southampton Railway Company routed their line through Basingstoke - well north of what would have been a more natural route - because they had plans to build a branch from Basingstoke to Bristol. The Bristol line was never built, although Basingstoke later became the junction for the LSWR line to Salisbury and Exeter. Basingstoke's original station, built by Sir William Tite, was similar to that at Micheldever. It was replaced by the station featured on this card in 1896. A century later, amid the glass and hi-tec bustle of twenty-first century Basingstoke, it is still there, hardly changed, and busier than ever.

6. Bishop's Waltham. The three-and-three-quarter-mile branch along the Hamble Valley from Botley to Bishop's Waltham opened in 1863. The station building may appear excessive for a town of just over 2,000 people, but the local brickworks was keen to promote its products. What better way to do it than by making the first building visitors to the town would see an exuberant showpiece of the brickmaker's art. One thing they could not do was encourage passengers to use the line. Even the railmotors introduced in 1904 were more than adequate for the number of passengers. The station closed in 1932, although goods traffic lingered on until 1962. Sadly, the station building has since been demolished to make way for a roundabout.

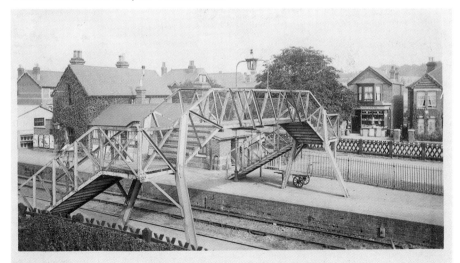

COSSER, PHOTO; SOUTHAMPTON.   Bitterne Station, Southampton.

7. Bitterne station (originally called Bitterne Road) was the first station on a branch opened in 1866 from St Denys to the Royal Victoria Military Hospital at Netley. In 1889, the line was extended to Fareham, giving passengers a direct route from Southampton to Portsmouth. Netley Hospital closed in 1958 and most of it has been demolished, but the branch is still open and forms part of an increasingly busy cross-country line from Portsmouth to Southampton and beyond. Bitterne station is still open and still looks much as it did a century ago, even down to the metal footbridge. Another card by Cosser.

8. Blackwater. The Blackwater River divides Hampshire from Berkshire. Near its banks stood the delightful wayside station of Blackwater, on the South Eastern & Chatham Railway's line from Redhill to Reading, which featured in Wilkie Collins' novel *The Woman in White*. Go there today and everything, apart from the rails and the platforms, has been swept away. A glass-and-metal shelter stands on each platform, a roadbridge has taken the place of the level crossing, and nothing in view is earlier than the 1960s.

9. Botley. In 1841, the London & Southampton Railway opened a branch from Eastleigh to Fareham and Gosport. The only intermediate station in the eleven miles between Eastleigh and Fareham was at Botley. In 1863, Botley became a junction when a branch was opened to Bishop's Waltham, three and a quarter miles away. Sometime early last century, the staff at Botley lined up in front of the station nameboard for a local postcard publisher. How many passengers would have wanted to buy a card showing the station staff is unknown, but at least the men featured on it probably accounted for a few sales. The Bishop's Waltham branch has long gone, but Botley is still open and still busy. In 1990, a station was opened at Hedge End, a mile to the north, to serve the rapidly growing business community.

725. CENTRAL STATION, BOURNEMOUTH.

10. Bournemouth Central. When a railway was built from Southampton to Dorchester in the 1840s, so few people lived on the coast that the line was routed inland through Ringwood. Twenty years later, the property developers had moved in and were busy turning a fishing village called Bournemouth into a fashionable resort. A branch line was opened from Ringwood to Bournemouth, but this soon proved inadequate, and in 1888 a new line was built through Bournemouth and on to Dorchester. The old inland line was downgraded and eventually closed in 1964. While the arrival of the railway was a major factor in Bournemouth's success, Bournemouth's residents were keen that it should not disturb their genteel resort, and the station was sited well inland. Bournemouth station, with its magnificent overall roof, has been recently restored, with palm trees growing on the site of the old central tracks through the station. A W.H. Smith postcard.

S 3705 WEST STATION, BOURNEMOUTH

11. Bournemouth West opened in 1874 as the terminus of a branch from Poole and the Somerset & Dorset Railway. It was here that generations of daytrippers from Bath and beyond arrived for a few hours by the sea. As it served the western residential area of the town and was closer to the pier and the town centre than Central station, many expresses from London were divided at Bournemouth Central, one portion going on to Weymouth, the other terminating at Bournemouth West. Bournemouth West closed in 1965 and the Wessex Way trunk road runs through the site. Another W.H. Smith postcard.

Bramley Station.

12. Bramley. The line from Reading to Basingstoke, now part of the inter-city line from the Midlands to the South Coast, is all that survives of the Great Western's attempts to reach the Hampshire coast. Opened in 1848, it was originally broad gauge, but was converted to mixed gauge in 1856 and to standard gauge in 1869. Although Bramley had a population of around 500, trains passed through without stopping for almost 50 years, before a station was opened in 1895. Apart from the lengthening of the platform on the left, the station is almost unchanged today.

THE RAILWAY STATION, BREAMORE.

13. Breamore (pronounced Bremmer), on the Salisbury-West Moors-Bournemouth line, opened in 1866 and closed, two years short of its centenary, in 1964. The brick-built station building on the left, with its corrugated iron canopy, is still there, hidden amid the undergrowth. The shelter on the other platform has gone, although its footings remain. The trackbed is a wilderness of brambles and small trees, a mini-nature reserve full of birdsong. Breamore station has simply been abandoned and, after 40 years of decay and dereliction, it is one of the most atmospheric railway sites in Hampshire. *"I expect you will remember this,"* ran the message on this postcard sent to Warminster in April 1905.

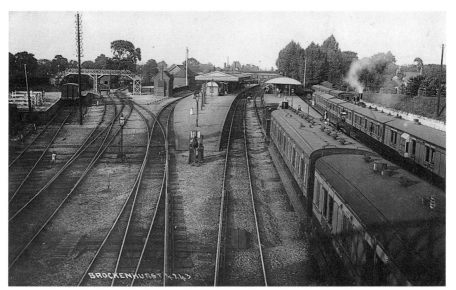

14. Brockenhurst. The railway arrived at Brockenhurst in 1847 and in time it became an important junction, with passengers changing for Lymington and the ferry to the Isle of Wight. Regular passengers included famous West Wight residents such Alfred Lord Tennyson and the photographer Julia Margaret Cameron, some of whose photographs adorn the waiting room walls. Although still busy, the station has seen many changes since this postcard was published. Many of the original buildings were replaced in the 1930s. The platforms and canopies have been extended and the line on the far right has gone. The goods yard on the left has been tarmacked over, its bridge demolished, and the goods shed turned into an Italian restaurant.

15. Bursledon, on the single track branch from St Denys to Netley, opened in 1889, the same year that the branch was extended to Fareham. As can be seen from this early twentieth century view, the line remained single for many years, but was eventually doubled to cope with increasing traffic. All the buildings in this picture have gone, a footbridge runs over to a platform on the left, and copious tree growth has hidden the houses on the hill. Out of view to the left is the Hamble River with its forest of yacht masts.

16. Chandler's Ford was on the LSWR's original route from London to Salisbury via Eastleigh and opened in 1847. When a direct route from Basingstoke to Salisbury was opened seven years later, the line through Chandler's Ford was downgraded to a branch. Passenger services were withdrawn in 1969, although the line stayed open for freight. On a visit to the station early in 2003, all that remained of the station were remnants of the platforms, hidden in undergrowth, with a single track running between them. Plans to re-open the station to passengers and re-introduce a shuttle service to Southampton, were advanced enough, however, for many of the trees and undergrowth in the old station yard to have been cleared away, and the station re-opened on 18th May 2003. Postcard published by Willsteed.

17. Eastleigh. When the railway between Southampton and Winchester opened in 1839, Eastleigh - originally known as Bishopstoke - was the only intermediate station. It served a small village, but when it became a junction, first for a line to Fareham and Gosport, and then for one to Romsey and Salisbury, the village started expanding. The *Junction Family Hotel* was built, and a large cheese market opened next to the station. In 1889, the LSWR bought a large plot of land by the line, opened a carriage and wagon works, and renamed the station Eastleigh. The old village was swamped by rows of terraced houses. In 1895, the old station was enlarged and its frontage extended outwards. A locomotive works was built in 1909. This view of Eastleigh station, familiar to generations of travellers, was transformed in the late twentieth century when the hotel and the 1895 frontage was swept away to provide a car park, thus restoring Tite's 1839 building to its rightful place at the entrance to the station.

18. Fareham station, on the line from Winchester to Gosport, opened in 1841. Later, it became an important junction and was rebuilt. It has, however, changed remarkably little since this postcard was published a century ago. Even the modern bike stand is in the same position as the bikes in the picture. The only significant difference is the removal of the covering on the footbridge.

19. Farnborough. When a station opened at Farnborough on the London & Southampton Railway in 1838, it served a village of less than 500 people. The establishment of an army camp between Aldershot and Farnborough in 1854, however, led to rapid expansion. By 1861, Farnborough's population had grown to 5,500 and, by the end of the nineteenth century, it was the largest town, apart from Aldershot, in north Hampshire. The establishment of His Majesty's Balloon Factory at Farnborough in 1905 was the start of the aeronautical connection which has made the town famous throughout the world. The town's station, rebuilt in the late nineteenth century when the line was quadrupled, has hardly changed since this card was published. The main difference, as at Fareham, is the removal of the covering on the footbridge.

20. Fawley. The Fawley branch was the last railway to be built in Hampshire. New railways may not have been much of a novelty by 1925, but even so the crowd which has turned out to greet the arrival of the first train looks rather sparse. The line was built to serve the Agwi oil refinery, opened in 1922. Passenger services were very much of an afterthought, put on mainly to take workers to and from the refinery. Passenger trains were withdrawn in 1966, but the refinery, taken over and rebuilt by Esso in 1951 as the largest in the world, has ensured the line's survival. Access to Fawley station to assess its present condition is impossible - unless you work for Esso, that is - for it is in the middle of the refinery and strictly off limits to all but official visitors.

21. Fleet station, originally known as Fleet Pond, opened in 1847, and was rebuilt when the line was quadrupled. The footbridge and the four tracks running through Fleet are still there, but the station buildings seen on this card have all been swept away and replaced by modern ones.

22. Fordingbridge. This early twentieth century postcard shows Fordingbridge station, dating from 1866, with a Bournemouth West-Salisbury train arriving. Although the road from which this picture was taken is still called Station Road, no trace of the station, or of the line that passed through it, remains. An animal feed factory occupies the site, and the trackbed beyond is covered with houses.

23. Fratton & Southsea station, still open and still busy (especially when Portsmouth are playing at nearby Fratton Park), has changed remarkably little since this card was published. To the left, out of shot, is Fratton Traincare Depot, on the site of the first few hundred yards of a branch to East Southsea, which opened in 1885 and succumbed to competition from trams in 1914.

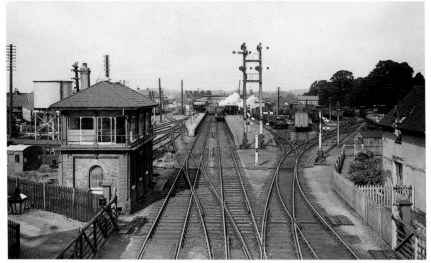

24. Havant. This view of Havant station from New Lane footbridge has changed enormously, although the signalbox (now somewhat extended) and the building on the right are still there. The tracks trailing off to the right have gone and the goods yards on both sides of the station have disappeared under car parks. In the 1930s the station was rebuilt, with two fast lines (one of which has since been lifted) flanked by two lines for stopping trains. Havant, dating from 1847, has a place in railway history as the venue, in 1858, for a pitched battle between employees and hired thugs of the LSWR and the LBSCR.

Hayling Island

25. Hayling Island. The branch from Havant to Hayling Island, dating from 1867, closed in 1963 because of the state of the wooden bridge across Langstone Harbour. Because of weight restrictions on the bridge, tiny, antiquated 'Terrier' locomotives, built at Brighton Works in the 1870s, were used on the line until the end, thus ensuring a steady trickle of railway enthusiasts in the line's last days. So much a part of the local scene were these diminutive engines that, when the line closed, Brickwood's Brewery bought one and put it outside a pub on the island. Most of the old station buildings at Hayling Island have gone, although the goods shed has found a new use as a theatre. The engine which once stood outside the pub has now found a new home on the Isle of Wight Steam Railway.

26 Herriard, deep in the countryside, was on the Basingstoke & Alton Light Railway, built by the LSWR in 1901 to stop the GWR building a line from Basingstoke to Portsmouth. Once built, it had achieved its purpose, and when the army called for rails to build lines in France in 1916, the LSWR was only too happy to rip up those between Basingstoke and Alton. In 1923, the Southern Railway, who had acquired the defunct line, applied to formally abandon it, but a campaign by local residents forced them to relay tracks and reinstate services. The Southern finally got permission to withdraw passenger services in 1932 and goods services four years later. The Basingstoke & Alton Railway would be totally forgotten today were it not for something which happened after closure which endears it to railway lovers worldwide - the filming of *Oh, Mr Porter* on the line in 1937.

Hinton Admiral Station

27. Hinton Admiral station, near the *Cat & Fiddle Inn* on the borders of the New Forest, has changed little since it was built in 1886. A new footbridge has been built, some of the fancy gabling on the red-brick station building has disappeared, an electricity sub-station has replaced the hut on the left, and pylons dominate the scene, but otherwise it still appears much as it did a century ago.

Hook Station.

T.H.
B.

28. A postcard published by Terry Hunt of **Hook**, between Farnborough and Basingstoke, was a relatively late addition to Hampshire's railway network, not opening until 1883, although trains had been passing through since 1839. Hook's island platform has long since been demolished and now buddleias sway where once it stood. The old red-brick buildings and extensive canopies still survive, but have a rundown, neglected appearance, very different to their spick and span appearance on this Edwardian postcard. But with this number of staff to take care of them, it is hardly surprising that Hook looked so smart.

HORSEBRIDGE

29. Horsebridge. Although the 'Sprat & Winkle' line from Andover to Romsey closed in 1964, a surprise awaits anyone who turns off the road near King's Somborne and heads down to the old station at Horsebridge - signals, a coach in the platform, and everything much as it looked when this card was published a century ago. Horsebridge station, with its own website (www.horsebridgestation.co.uk) has been lovingly restored as a corporate entertainment centre. Although trains will never again thread down this part of the Test valley, their memory is kept alive by this unique tribute to the past.

30. Hythe. The arrival of the first passenger train at Hythe, on 25 July 1925, seems to have caused as little excitement as it did at Fawley. None of the small group who turned up to witness it even managed to raise a smile. Passenger services ended in 1966, but Hythe station is still there, behind a high-security fence, with a sign announcing that it is a heritage centre, and oil trains still run through. The main railway interest at Hythe, however, is the wonderful pier tramway, built for a mustard gas factory at Avonmouth in the Great War, moved to Hythe in 1922 and hardly changed since.

31. Itchen Abbas opened in 1865 when a line was opened from Alton to Winchester. When British Railways closed the line in 1973, a preservation society stepped in, but, although they managed to acquire the Alton-Alresford section (now known as the Watercress Line), they had to give up plans for the remaining section into Winchester. Itchen Abbas, on the bit they didn't save, has since been bulldozed to make way for houses.

32. Swanwick. It was not difficult to decide which card should form the centrepiece of this I background, little changed today, except that part of it is now an Indian restaurant) is incide surrounding countryside queue with their loads of freshly-picked strawberries, while special tra was of the essence, lest luscious mouth-watering delicacies should turn into mouldy mush. Bas can be seen on the left of the picture. To give some idea how important the strawberry season w it is all a distant memory. The sidings have been ripped up and turned into a car park and strav

vonderful view of Swanwick at strawberry-time won hands down. The station itself (in the
activity going on in the foreground. Down the dusty approach, carts and wagons from the
speed them on the next stage of their journey. In an age before widespread refrigeration, time
them were made in the sheds next to the station yard - the corner of one, which still survives,
vick, in one week in 1931, one and a quarter million baskets were sent from the station. Today,
illed, cling-film packed, air-freighted, and generally tasteless, are available all the year round.

33. King's Worthy, on the Didcot, Newbury & Southampton Railway, was brand new when this card was published, only having opened in 1909. The line, which had been there since 1885, was intended as part of a trunk route between the Midlands and the South, but, like the Midland & South Western Junction Railway from Cheltenham to Andover, it never got beyond the branch-line stage. Its moment of glory came in 1943, when, in the run-up to D Day, it was upgraded to handle the large numbers of troops and equipment being sent down to the South Coast. After the war, it slumped back into the doldrums. It closed in 1960, and now the platforms at King's Worthy lie under the A34.

34. Lee-on-Solent. The branch from Fort Brockhurst, north of Gosport, to the rising resort of Lee-on-Solent opened in 1894. Unfortunately it did not rise far enough to justify a railway service, and the line closed in 1931. Its passing went almost unnoticed, a total of six men and a dog travelling on the last train. Today the station at Lee-on-Solent houses an amusement arcade.

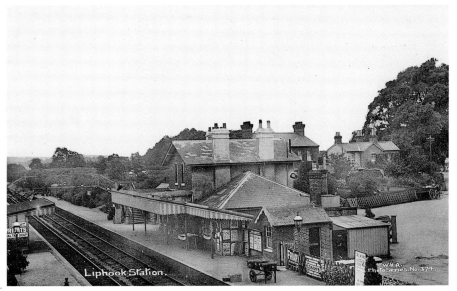

35. Liphook. Portsmouth had to wait until 1847 for a railway - six years after Gosport - and even then Pomponians had to put up with a circuitous journey via Eastleigh or Brighton until a direct line opened twelve years later. This passed through the delightful, but very hilly, countryside between Havant and Godalming. Gradients were severe, curves tight, and initially the line was single track. The station serving the little country town of Liphook, near the Hampshire-Surrey border, has hardly changed since this card was published. Just about the only substantial difference is the replacement of the wooden shed on the right with something more modern.

36. Liss. Next stop down the line from Liphook is Liss. Unlike Liphook, it has seen many changes since this card was published. While the building on the left-hand platform survives, all those on the right have gone, to be replaced by a modern glass building. A new footbridge spans the tracks and new crossing gates have been added.

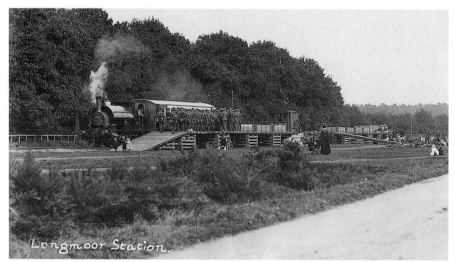

Longmoor Station.

37. Longmoor. An army camp was opened at Longmoor after the Boer war. In 1905, a narrow gauge railway was built from Longmoor to Bordon so that the camp could be extended. This line was later converted to standard gauge to form the Woolmer Instructional Military Railway, where soldiers could be taught how to build and operate railways. This line was eventually extended to Liss and renamed the Longmoor Military railway. At its peak, there were over 70 miles of track at Longmoor and a passenger service was run for army personnel. After the Second World War, the railway declined in importance. It closed completely in 1969. There were hopes that part of it could be re-opened as a heritage railway, and various preserved locomotives were kept on the site for a time, but the plans came to nothing.

38. Longparish. The Hurstbourne-Fullerton Junction line, opened in 1885, was, like the Basingstoke-Alton line, a spoiler - this time to ward off plans by the Didcot, Newbury & Southampton Railway, backed by the GWR, to open a branch from Whitchurch to Bournemouth. The discrepancy between the size of Longparish station and the size of the railmotor standing at the platform tells us everything we need to know about the fortunes of this line. Originally double track, it was singled in 1913, closed to passengers in 1931 and closed completely in 1956. The station is now a private house.

39. Lymington Town station, built in 1860, is a very pleasing exercise in the Italianate style. Particularly interesting, to the architecturally inclined, is the slotting of a pair of Italianate windows into a single relieving arch, picked out in different coloured brick. Although a flat-roofed extension has been added to the right of the building and part of the wall at the front has been reconstructed, the station is remarkably unchanged today. The goods buildings on the left, however, have given way to examples of late twentieth century trading-estate monolithism and a bus depot occupies the site where the photographer stood to take this picture.

40. Lymington Pier. In 1884, the Lymington branch was extended across the river to a new station at Lymington Pier, from where Alfred Lord Tennyson could hop onto the ferry to Yarmouth. The view today looks very different. The run-round loop went with the demise of steam, and, although the platform is longer, it has lost its canopy. Waiting passengers have to make do with bus-stop-style shelters. The biggest difference, though, is the size of the ships. Paddle steamers have given way to ferries which tower high above the shuttle trains from Brockenhurst.

41. Lyndhurst Road. Now renamed Ashurst (New Forest), Lyndhurst Road station, dating from 1847, is still open, with fast services to Waterloo throughout the day. Much has changed, however, since this card was published. The buildings on the far platform have been replaced by a bus shelter, the canopies have gone, the footbridge has been replaced by one in metal, and, although the station house (just out of view to the right) is still there, it is in private hands, and the station is unstaffed.

42. Medstead. The Alton-Winchester line opened in 1865. Three years later, pressure from local residents led to this functional red-brick station being built at Medstead. British Railways closed the line in 1973, but Medstead station has seen a new lease of life as an intermediate stop on the Watercress Line.

43. Micheldever (known as Andover Road until 1856) dates from the opening of the London & Southampton railway in 1840. Much has changed since this card was published. Tite's yellow-brick building, on the left, now stands guard over a trackless platform. The platform and the buildings on the right have completely disappeared. Passengers still enter the station from the left and have to walk down a subway to get to the island platform. Micheldever is, as it always has been, in the middle of nowhere. But it is the railhead for a wide area. Nothing better emphasises the emptiness of much of inland Hampshire than the fact that Micheldever is the only station in the 19 miles between Basingstoke and Winchester.

44. New Milton. The tidy brick-built station at New Milton, with the date 1886 over the entrance, is similar to many others on the Bournemouth direct line. Apart from the loss of the wooden railings on the canopy above the booking office entrance and the discoloration of the bricks by lichen, little has changed since this card was published. The house in the background has lost its gables, but the crenellated water tower behind it still dominates the area.

Nursling Station.

45. Nursling. The wayside station at Nursling, four and a half miles north of Southampton, opened in 1882. It was some distance from the village it was intended to serve, and lack of custom led to closure in 1957. The red-brick station house still survives, with a pigeon loft where the drive once stood, but everything else - platforms, shelters, fencing - has been swept away. The M27 crosses the line in the background.

Oakley Station.

46. Oakley. One of the most inexplicable losses among Hampshire's stations is Oakley, on the main line between Basingstoke and Salisbury, which closed in 1963. Trains still run through, but the station building, dating from 1854, is now a carpet warehouse. Although it is some way out of the village, there are periodic calls for it to be re-opened, but it is so expensive to build a new station these days, because of Health & Safety and other regulations, that Oakley's early return to the rail network seems unlikely.

903.   PETERSFIELD STATION

Goodes, Petersfield

47. Petersfield, on the direct line from London to Portsmouth, opened in 1859. Five years later it became the junction for a branch to Midhurst. Like the stations on the Salisbury-Exeter line such as Axminster, built around the same time, it is a good example of Tite's Tudor Gothic period. The Midhurst line has long gone, but Petersfield station is still open and looks much as it did a century ago. The signals and the lines on the right have gone, but, apart from that, things appear much the same.

48. Pokesdown. Originally known as Boscombe, Pokesdown station opened in 1886. At first it consisted of an island platform reached by a flight of steps from the bridge in the background. In the 1920s, as the popularity of Bournemouth grew and more trains were required, it was decided to rebuild Pokesdown with four tracks, so that expresses could overtake stopping services. This view shows work in progress, with the island platform still in use, but new outer platforms - the down one needing massive shoring-up operations - nearing completion. A new booking hall was built to the left of the row of buildings in the background, with a footbridge for passengers to cross to the up platform. Today, the fast tracks, which were laid where the island platform once stood, have gone and only the slow lines remain.

Railway Station, Portchester.

49. Portchester station opened in 1848. Built of knapped flint, and looking like an outpost of Portchester Castle, it is a little gem. For many years, its main source of revenue came from daytrippers visiting the pleasure grounds at the castle. Today, daytrippers have given way to commuters, and the station is boarded up and rather down-at-heel - a sad fate for such an unusual building.

50. Portsmouth & Southsea. The railway reached Portsmouth in 1848, and the original station was, according to a history of the LSWR written in 1883, *"a miserable structure."* Its replacement, built in 1876 when the line to the Harbour station was opened, was a complete contrast. Its chateau-like frontage, recalling that of Netley Hospital, in which Italianate design jostles with French decorative flourishes, makes it one of the most striking examples of late nineteenth century railway architecture in the country, and one of Portsmouth's most memorable buildings. It is also unusual in having tracks on two levels - a lower-level terminus, behind the imposing facade, and a high-level station, from which this view was taken, used by trains carrying on to the Harbour.

S 5053   PORTSMOUTH HARBOUR STATION & PIER.

51. Portsmouth Harbour. The wooden-platformed station at Portsmouth Harbour has a distinctly nautical feel. Built on a jetty, with the water washing beneath it, it opened in 1876. During the Second World War, it was a target for German bombers. It was nearly destroyed early in 1941 and was closed for six weeks while repairs were carried out. Eventually, the old station was rebuilt in the late twentieth century. This was another postcard published by W.H. Smith.

52. Privett. The Meon Valley Railway from Alton to Fareham, which opened in 1903, was, like the Basingstoke & Alton Light Railway, built to block the GWR's plans for a line from Basingstoke to Portsmouth. Its arts-and-crafts inspired stations were, like the one at Privett, on an expansive scale, out of all proportion to the size of the communities served or the level of services provided. The line closed in 1955, but several of the stations, such as the one at Privett, have been imaginatively restored as private houses.

53. Romsey. The ravages of the twentieth century have had little effect on the yellow-brick station at Romsey, dating from 1847. The only significant difference between the view on this card and the view today is the fencing on the left, which has been replaced by something more modern.

Rook's Series 1 Railway Station, Rowland's Castle

54. Rowland's Castle is the rural station par excellence. When it opened in 1859, the village only had about 300 inhabitants, and, although it has grown somewhat, little has changed at the station since this card was published a century ago. A new footbridge, south of the station buildings, has replaced the old one, but a traveller from a century and a half ago would have little difficulty recognising the spot today.

55. St Denys. In 1861, the LSWR opened a small station north of Southampton to serve the village of Portswood. Five years later, when a branch was opened to the Royal Victoria Military Hospital at Netley, a new, and much larger, Portswood station, complete with Italianate station building by Sir William Tite, opened at the junction. In 1876 the new station was renamed St Denys. It is still open and Tite's building still stands, albeit with a by-pass roaring past its shuttered doors.

56. Sholing station, on the Netley branch, opened in 1866, but was not thought worthy of the fine Italianate buildings that graced other stations on the branch. The wooden buildings seen on this card survived until at least the early 1980s (albeit in a rather dilapidated state), but have since been demolished. All that remains today is the footbridge.

57. Southampton Docks. The railway reached Southampton in 1839, and Tite's Italianate terminus opened a year later. With its rusticated arcade at street level, it somehow manages to look as much like a theatre as a railway station. Tite adopted a similar layout when he designed his most famous station, Carlisle, seven years later. Carlisle, however, was in Tudor Gothic style, a reflection of how styles in station building had changed. This one was Southampton's only station until 1847 and remained its principal station until 1895, when the more important through trains started calling at the new Southampton West station instead. It entered a period of slow decline, which ended in closure in 1966. It now houses a casino.

Southampton West Station.   jws 828

58. Southampton West. The history of Southampton West is a complex one, involving no less than five re-buildings. When the line from Southampton to Dorchester opened in 1847, a makeshift halt was opened at Blechynden Terrace. Three years later, a station, called Blechynden, opened. In 1858, a new spur opened, enabling trains from London to Dorchester to by-pass the original Southampton station and call at Blechynden instead. In keeping with its new-found status, Blechynden was rebuilt and renamed Southampton West End. The opening of the direct line to Bournemouth in 1888 brought further traffic, and, in 1895, having outgrown the original site, Southampton West End was rebuilt on a new site to the west. This station was again rebuilt in 1935 and in 1966. This postcard show the station as it appeared after its move to the 1895 site, complete with the tower, which was demolished in 1966. Postcard published by J. Welch & Sons.

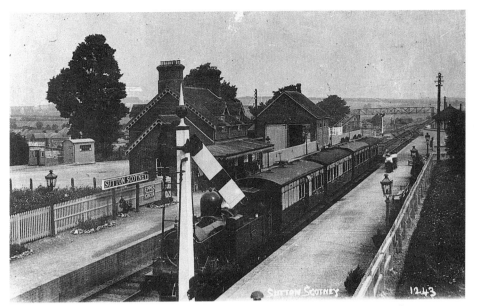

59. Sutton Scotney. A wonderful panoramic shot of a train calling at Sutton Scotney, on the Didcot, Newbury & Southampton Railway. The line closed in 1960. Today, there is no trace of the platforms and a derelict and unlovely light industrial unit occupies the spot where the station buildings once stood. All that remains is the goods shed, converted to industrial use, but now also derelict. The site looks ripe for re-development, and no doubt one day soon, executive houses will spring up where once the milk train whistled on its way.

60. Sway, on the borders of the New Forest, has changed little since this card was published. The signalbox and the hut on the left have gone, the station building has been extended, but Sway station, with a sofa in the booking hall and an eclectic collection of objects in its waiting room, would still be recognisable to its Edwardian patrons today.

61. Swaythling, between Eastleigh and Southampton, opened in 1883. At the time, there were plans to quadruple the tracks through here - hence the gap between the station building and the platform. The plans, however, came to nothing, and, apart from the loss of the inn on the right, and its replacement by new houses, the scene looks much the same today.

TISTED STATION.

62. Tisted. Like Privett, Tisted looked as though it was an important station on a main line, instead of a sleepy passing place on a rural branch line. Opened in 1903 and closed in 1955, it has, like Privett, been converted to a private house. Unlike Privett, however, railway signs and enamel advertisements adorn its walls, and an old British Railways coach stands at the platform. A tank engine of World War One vintage once stood there as well, but in 1998 it was lifted out by crane and taken to a new home on a steam railway in Northamptonshire.

Tott☐n 3tation, near Southampton.

63. **Totton** station (originally known as Eling Junction) opened in 1859. The station building, probably designed by Tite, is a very pleasing example of the Tudor Cottage style which, by this time, had replaced the classicism of the buildings on the London & Southampton Railway of 20 years earlier. The shelter on the left-hand platform has gone, but the station building, complete with its canopy, still survives, as does the mill in the background. Another postcard published by Cosser of Southampton.

64. **Warblington.** The introduction of railmotors in the early twentieth century meant that low-cost, low-maintenance halts could be opened to serve villages and suburbs. One such was Warblington, on the outskirts of Havant. Originally known as Denvilles, it opened in 1907. The halt is still open today, although, almost inevitably, its surroundings have changed beyond all recognition. The large trees have gone, and houses have spring up on both sides of the road. The crossing-keeper's house has disappeared and the only point of continuity between then and now is the chimney of the house in the distance just above the left-hand crossing gates.

65. West Meon. The Meon Valley line, which owed its existence to a determination to keep the GWR out of Hampshire, was an appallingly difficult line to build, cutting as it did across some of the hilliest parts of the county. As well as two long tunnels, there was a tall, three-arched viaduct on the line at West Meon. It was the poor condition of this which led to the line's closure in 1955, but, even had it been in perfect condition, it is unlikely that the line would have lasted much longer. The station, like the viaduct, was demolished after the line closed and there is little, except for odd cuttings and embankments, to indicate a railway once ran through this part of the county.

66. Weyhill, north of Andover on the Midland & South Western Junction Railway, opened in 1882. After passenger services were withdrawn in 1961, the line was kept open as far as Ludgershall for freight. A disused, rusting track still runs through Weyhill, but the station has long since disappeared. All that remains is the old stationmaster's house, now privately owned.